Early Christmas

Bobbie Kalman

The Early Settler Life Series

Crabtree Publishing Company

To Peter

Special thanks to *Nancy Cook, Andrea Crabtree, Judie Ellis, Samantha Crabtree and Stephanie Williams.*

Copyright © 1981, 1990, 1991 Crabtree Publishing Company

Cataloging in Publication Data

Kalman, Bobbie, 1947 –
* Early Christmas*

(Early settler life series)
Includes index.
ISBN   0-86505-001-5 hardcover
ISBN   0-86505-003-1 paperback

1. Christmas – History.
I. Title. II. Series

GT 4985.K34   394.2'68282' 097   C81-094117-1
LC93-27349

350 Fifth Ave, Suite 3308
New York, NY 10118

R.R. #4
360 York Road
Niagara-on-the-Lake, ON
Canada L0S 1J0

73 Lime Walk
Headington, Oxford 0X3 7AD
United Kingdom

Contents

Making a new home in the wilderness was hard work. People had no time to celebrate Christmas.

The plum pudding held the spirit of Christmas for the new settler.

Our Christmas has changed over the years

Christmas in the very early days of our country was little like the Christmas we know today. The customs that are so much a part of today's Christmas were not even known to the first settlers. Santa Claus, Christmas stockings, Christmas trees and Christmas cards all came to North America long after the first settlers had arrived.

A lonely Christmas for men

The very first Christmases in the New World were often celebrated by men alone. Many men came by themselves to make new lives. They were young men who were not yet married. Sometimes husbands came first and their families followed them later. Men worked as trappers and loggers in the woods. Their Christmas celebrations were simple, if they celebrated at all. No matter how little these men had, they often managed to make a plum pudding. The Christmas pudding seemed to contain the spirit of Christmas for the new settlers. Years later the Christmas tree took over as the new symbol of Christmas.

No time for Christmas at first

The first families who settled in the New Land had to work nearly all the time just to stay alive. There were trees to be chopped down, houses to be built, crops to be planted and roads to be made. Often these settlers couldn't do anything special for Christmas because they had nothing more than the bare necessities of life.

More time to celebrate later

Christmas became more important as people became more settled. Families and friends made special efforts to be together during the Christmas season. It was the one time of the year when there was not as much work to be done. The harvest was finished and new planting was months away.

The Christmas of the late eighteenth and early nineteenth century meant lots of parties for adults. There were no special celebrations for children yet.

Christmas for adults

The late eighteenth century and early nineteenth century Christmases were important family and social times. Christmas in those days meant family get-togethers, parties, dancing, parlor games, outdoor fun, weddings and, of course, a huge dinner ending with a plum pudding.

Early Christmas was a special occasion for adults. There were no celebrations for children yet. Children sometimes received a few home-made gifts, but gift-giving was not yet an important part of Christmas.

Christmas for kids

Christmas changed into a Christmas for children during the second half of the nineteenth century, between 1850 and 1900. About one hundred and thirty years ago, people started putting up Christmas trees, hanging stockings and waiting for Santa Claus to bring gifts.

Our Christmas today grew out of the Christmases of the early settlers. It is still the most special time of the year because the spirit and pride of the settler, that once was symbolized in the flaming plum pudding, still lives on in the sparkling lights of the Christmas tree today.

Christmas wouldn't be Christmas without plum pudding, even if you are trapping deep in the bush. These men are steaming their pudding in an old rag. The pudding will remind them of Christmas with their families.

Christmas in the wilderness

Often it was necessary for the early settlers to work at extra jobs in the winter. Some of the men had to work in the woods as loggers or trappers. Most of the time these men were alone in the woods for many months. They looked forward to celebrating Christmas because it reminded them of their families and friends. It gave the men in the woods a feeling of being part of a civilized world.

After the many hardships these men had, Christmas was a good excuse to relax and have a little fun. Some of the men were lucky enough to have Christmas at a fur trading post. The men who stayed in the bush hunted a deer or a moose and roasted it for their Christmas meal. No matter how little they had in the way of food, many of the men managed to make a Christmas pudding. Without it, Christmas just would not have been Christmas!

The Hudson's Bay Company governed large tracts of land in what is now Canada and the United States. Native People, trappers, voyageurs (paddlers of large cargo canoes), storekeepers and soldiers all celebrated Christmas together. This is Fort Garry.

Christmas at a fur trading post

Christmas was a special occasion at the trading post. The main meeting room was painted in stripes of bright colors. People came to the Christmas dinner in their best clothes. The dinner was served at two o'clock in the afternoon in the newly-decorated meeting room.

There were no tablecloths. The plates were made of tin. The smiles on the happy faces of the guests reflected in the shiny plates. A whole cow was usually roasted for Christmas dinner. There were also platters filled with fish and poultry. The foods which made this dinner different from other Christmas dinners were boiled buffalo hump, dried moose nose, smoked buffalo tongue and beaver tail. Buffalo calf, taken from the stomach of the mother buffalo, was the biggest treat of the dinner, next to the plum pudding. There were mountains of vegetables and bread on the tables. And, there was the pudding!

In the evening there was a dance. All the people who lived at the post were invited. Many Native People came. The Native People dressed in their best clothes for the dance. Everyone danced in different ways. People spoke many different languages.

All the guests had a wonderful time and left the party in a good mood. Spirits were high! People were again ready to face the hardships of the wilderness for another new year.

A jolly Christmas load

'Twas cold outside, an' so, says I
I can rest me, now the chores is done,
The wind is sharp; there's a threatenin' sky
A snow-storm's just begun.

I gave the logs a livenin' poke,
An' settled down for an easy spell,
My cider near, an' my pipe to smoke,
The fire a-burnin' well.

When all at once I thinks to myself
Of the parson's dues I'd ought to pay,
A-lyin' there on the chimney shelf
I got the last today.

So out I went. The old ox team
Was standin' there on the nigh cross-road.
You should ha' seen them critters steam;
The wind it sang and blowed.

So off I went.'Twas precious slow.
I gave the parson his quarter's pay.
"I'm glad to get it", says he; "you know
To-morrer's Christmas Day."

I kissed his young'uns, said goodbye,
An' back I started the other half,
When all at once - may I hope to die
Ef I didn't hear a laugh!

"Hello!" says I, a-turnin' round;
"Who be ye, sir?" an' I up an' smiled,
For there was standin' on the ground
The smallest little child.

He laughed again. "I want a ride.
I'm not alone; can you take us all?
Can you take me in and the rest beside?"
I grinned. "Twill be a haul."

So I packed 'em every one.
I tell ye what, 'twas a jolly load.
'Twas no time going, with all the fun;
We's home before we knowed.

Ma stood a-waitin' at the door;
An' Sally cried, "Why the darlin' things!"
An' kissed 'em all, while I said, "Oh Lor'
D'you see? They've all got wings!"

It stumped me so I laughed out loud,
When, lo'n'behold! th'hull thing was gone-
The old ox team, an' the jolly crowd -
An' I woke up some forlorn.

But ma said, when I told my dream,
"Well folks don't reckon the loads they brings
You took your'n cheerful, an' so, t'd seem,
You saw your blessin's wings."

A settler's dream

This old poem was written over a hundred years ago. Some of the words may seem strange to you. The language is a country "dialect". It is a different way of speaking a language. The poem is written exactly the way it would have been spoken. Make a list of the words which are new to you and look them up in your dictionary.

The settler in the poem dreams of finding a load of angels in his sleigh. He is sad to find them gone when he wakes up. He enjoyed their company so much! His mother cheers him up by telling him that the dream meant that he was the type of person who did his jobs with a smile, no matter how heavy the load was. He was a happy person!

9

"Soon the whole house looked and smelled like the outdoors!"

A settler's first Christmas

Ann Elizabeth Walker lived in a farmhouse in the backwoods of Peterboro. She had arrived from England less than a year ago with her family. She missed her old friends terribly! The closest neighbors to her new home were two-and-a-half miles away. The early December weather was so cold, that she did not even feel like going out. She usually went for a walk with her brother John and sister Edith at this time each day. They all enjoyed the new adventure of walking on snowshoes through the woods. However, Ann Elizabeth was feeling sad today. She thought about old Decembers in England when she and her friends were busy preparing for Christmas. Their homes would be decked out in mistletoe and holly. Friends came to call almost every day.

Too busy for Christmas

Since she had arrived in the New World, her family had done nothing but work to clear the land of trees, build their house and plant the wheat and vegetables they would eat. There seemed to be no time for fun in this new land. Their neighbors did not talk of Christmas plans. She had heard that children even went to school on Christmas day! Ann Elizabeth did not know if she could stand a new life that was all work and no play!

Christmas after all!

Mrs. Walker must have read her daughter's mind. She asked the family to sit down. She wanted to discuss Christmas plans with them.

"I just received a letter at the General Store", she said. "Your Uncle Marc and Aunt Caroline Crabtree are coming to spend Christmas with us."

There was instant joy on the faces of the children. They would celebrate Christmas after all! And, they would get to see their cousins Andrea, Peter and Alison!

Battles in the snow

Ann Elizabeth hugged her mother. "Let's go into the woods for some ever-greens", she suggested. "There are some cranberry bushes nearby", said her mother. "The berries look close enough to holly berries."

They bundled up and ran outdoors, still in high spirits. John threw a snowball and hit Ann Elizabeth right in the nose! The war was on! Edith and Ann Elizabeth jumped John and scrubbed his face with handfuls of snow. Mr. Walker stopped the battle and reminded them of the job they set out to do. They all hopped on the ox-cart and headed into the bush.

Outdoors indoors!

The next day the whole family decorated the house with evergreens, cranberries and ribbons. They hung branches, wreaths and garlands over doorways and around the walls. Soon the whole house smelled and looked like the outdoors! The Walkers had never felt cosier in their new home!

Prowling the pantry

Mrs. Walker and Ann Elizabeth planned the Christmas dinner. There was not much fancy food in the pantry, but they decided that Christmas dinner would be wonderful, no matter what! They put aside the best vegetables and fruit preserves. The goose, which was being fattened, would become the Christmas goose. Mother and daughter searched the pantry for ingredients for the Christmas pudding. They found some currants and decided to add some of the berries they had found in the bush. The pantry was low on spices and other ingredients, but they found enough to make a big, fat pudding. Everyone stirred the pudding. They made a wish as they stirred. The pudding was left to age in the pot until Christmas day.

Fun on Christmas Eve

The day before Christmas arrived and so did the Crabtrees. Oh what happiness there was among the children! That night everyone sang songs and carols. They swapped stories and played games. Uncle

Mother brings in the big fat plum pudding!

Marc made the children scream in a game of Blind Man's Bluff. John, Edith and Ann Elizabeth could hardly sleep, they were so excited!

Christmas Day arrives

After the church service the next day, the Walkers and Crabtrees sat down to their Christmas meal. Mrs. Walker and Ann Elizabeth had cooked a gigantic goose. Mrs. Crabtree had brought some boiled pork and mince pies.

The faces of the children lit up as their mother brought in the best part of the Christmas dinner, the big, fat, plum pudding! Everyone had more than enough to eat. They thanked God for their food and for the chance to be together.

Falling in snow

The children dashed outside to play in the snow. Mr. Walker had made them a sled. They could hardly wait to join some friends at the big hill. They slid and rolled down the hill. They fell into the snowbanks as the sleds bumped and flipped into the air.

Falling in love

Ann Elizabeth sat by the window, hoping that her neighbors, the Stells, would drop by for tea. She wanted to kiss their son Charles under the *kissing bough*. But it was growing dark already. It was probably too late for the Stells to come. Wait! What was that sound? Sleigh bells! The Stells' sleigh was coming up the road towards their house! Charles came in the door and gave Ann Elizabeth a big kiss under the bough. Christmas was complete!

The best Christmas ever

The Walkers' first Christmas in their new home was the best they had ever celebrated. It was not filled with as many parties as their past Christmases in England, but it was much more special. They learned how important they were to each other. They looked forward to their new lives in this new land. They decided that they would always celebrate Christmas, no matter how hard they had to work to survive here!

"I'll get you, John!"

THE TOP OF THE HILL. "STARTING THE BOBS."

"A SINGLE SKIPPER"

"AN OBJECT OF ENVY."

"THE BIG JOUNCE"

They fell into the snowbanks as the sleds bumped and flipped into the air.

13

These settlers decorate the village church with garlands of evergreens. Most of the settlers were Christians. Going to church was an important part of Christmas.

Jesus Christ was born on Christmas Day. We celebrate Christmas to remember His birthday. Jesus received gifts from kings and shepherds on His birthday. These children receive gifts on Christmas Day in celebration of Jesus' birthday.

Jesus Christ was born on Christmas Day!

Christmas celebrates the birth of Jesus Christ. Jesus Christ was born nearly two thousand years ago in a town called Bethlehem. His father was a carpenter named Joseph. His mother's name was Mary. Mary and Joseph were Jewish. The land in which they lived was ruled by the Romans at that time. The Roman ruler wanted all the Jews to go to the town in which they were born to be counted and taxed. Joseph and Mary had to go, even though Mary was almost ready to give birth to a baby.

When Joseph and Mary arrived in Bethlehem, they found that all the inns were full. There was not a bed to be found anywhere in the city. A kind man allowed Mary and Joseph to use his stable, so that they might at least have a roof over their heads. It was in this stable that Jesus Christ was born!

A star appeared in the sky and shone over the stable where Jesus lay. Some shepherds saw the star and came to greet the baby Jesus. They brought Him small gifts. Three kings also came searching for the new king who was to show men the way to God. They brought Jesus gifts of incense and gold.

Most of the early settlers were Christians. They went to church at Christmas to thank God for sending His son to earth to help His people. Christmas is a happy time for Christians. Jesus Christ was born that day!

Christmas celebrations often took place in the streets of the early towns.

Christmas in an early town

In the early towns, Christmas was often a time for rowdy activities. There was drinking, cock-fighting and sleigh-racing. Christmas was a time to let loose and forget all the hard work of making a new home in a new country.

People who lived in the early towns were closer to their neighbors than those who made their homes on the frontiers. It was easy for these townspeople to get from house to house. Many parties and balls were held during the Christmas season. While these people danced and partied, others who had just arrived at their plot of land in the bush had to work night and day to build their new home in the wilderness. With each new Christmas, new towns sprang up in what used to be the forest. As more people settled the land and opened shops in the towns, their Christmases grew into fancier events.

This new settler family celebrates Christmas alone. Their nearest neighbors live many miles away.

Many parties and balls were held during the Christmas season in the early towns.

Christmas fun in a pioneer village

Grandmother teaches the art of making pomanders to her grandchildren.

Pomanders for presents

The pioneers who lived in villages or on farms made their own fun and presents for Christmas.

Pomanders made popular home-made presents. They kept the house smelling pretty all year. Here is how to make them.

Take apples, oranges, lemons or limes. (Apples were most often used by the settlers, but citrus fruits have a stronger, fresher scent.) Stick the fruit full of cloves. The fruit should be only barely seen through the cloves. Roll the fruit in a mixture of cinnamon, allspice, orris root, cardamon and ginger. Tie the coated fruit with two shiny red or green satin ribbons. Hang to dry.

Your pomanders will make someone's room or closet smell beautiful all year! You can be sure that your gift will hang around and remind someone of you every time that person takes a breath.

These corn husk dolls will bring a lot of joy to some lucky pioneer girl.

This young settler makes a Christmas Crib from straw, wool, evergreens and wood.

Kissing boughs made of evergreens, apples and ribbons have the same power as mistletoe. They can bring kisses!

Peaceful night, silent night

The following Christmas carol is a version of "Silent Night" that the early settlers in this picture are singing. Learn the verses and sing them to the tune you know well!

Peaceful night! hallowed night!
All around, sleep profound
Whilst the happy and privileg'd pair
Watch the wonderful infant with care,
Sunk in heav'nly repose,
Sunk in heav'nly repose.

Peaceful night! hallowed night!
Shepherds first, tending sheep.
Angels' songs with wonder hear,
Sounding loud from far and near,
Jesus the Savior is come!
Jesus the Savior is come!

Peaceful night! hallowed night!
Son of God, O what love
Is in every feature portray'd!
Thou to us salvation art made,
Jesus the Savior of man!
Jesus the Savior of man!

These village carolers sing "Peaceful Night" in front of the church. Join in!

Evelyn stands guard at the door. Susie holds the lamp. Caroline and Peter get busy with their nasty deed. Uncle Harry will soon find prickly holly between his sheets!

Before the Christmas tree

The first settlers had their choice of end-less evergreens for Christmas decorations. Mistletoe and holly could not be found in the more northern climates but cranberries were a good substitute for the red holly berries. Many people who lived near towns or cities could buy holly or mistletoe in shops. But others made the best of what the nearby forest had to offer. There were lots of evergreens there!

Most of the early settler's time was spent chopping trees. Christmas was the one time of the year when everyone had fun doing it. The men chopped the trees and the women made decorations from the branches. Children also enjoyed gathering boughs for Christmas decorations. The custom of decorating Christmas trees started many years later. Only the branches of the evergreen trees were used in these early days.

Everyone enjoyed decorating for Christmas. Garlands and wreaths were hung all over the parlor. Christmas trees were not yet a part of Christmas.

These young boys worked all afternoon gathering boughs for Christmas decorations.

Christmas was a family time

Winter was the best time to travel. The sleighs and carioles could easily glide along the snow, even through the forest. Good travel allowed people to visit family and friends who lived on nearby farms or in nearby towns or cities.

The family above is heading for grandfather's house in the city to spend Christmas Eve there. The crisp night air is filled with the music of sleighbells jingling through the snow.

22

Grandmother meets her newest grandson for the first time.

These children are delighted with the gifts their grandfather brought. Does he look like someone else who brings presents?

The whole family gathers for Christmas.

Everyone scrambles to get away from the person who is "it" in blindman's bluff. If he guesses who you are, you are "it".

Parlor games, pantomimes and spooks!

Christmas was a time for indoor and outdoor games. The indoor games were called *Parlor Games*. The parlor was the room in the house used for entertaining guests. It was like a living room. Parlor games were like the games we now play at birthday parties. Charades and blindman's bluff were favorites. People also played guessing games, board games, such as backgammon and checkers, and card games.

Some of the parlor games were even dangerous. One game called for the person who was "it" to try to blow out a candle while blindfolded. The other players then moved the candle around away from the person who was trying to blow it out.

They directed the blindfolded player towards the candle with "cold and warm" clues. When the person felt his chin sizzle, the player knew it was "hot" and time to blow with all his or her might.

Each Christmas issue of a magazine or newspaper carried at least one gruesome ghost story. Ghost stories were told late on Christmas Eve, usually by candlelight. Stories written by Charles Dickens were also very popular. He wrote a Christmas story each year, which appeared in both British and North American papers. His most famous story "A Christmas Carol" is still one of the best loved Christmas stories of today.

Many city people went to concerts and pantomime plays on Christmas Eve.

A favorite activity on Christmas Eve was telling scary stories in the dark. With only a candle flickering, it was easy to believe any ghost story! Ghost stories were told late, just before people went to bed. Instead of having beautiful thoughts of Santa, these children shook with fright under their covers, thinking of prowling ghosts.

25

The proud and hardy settlers love the snow and ice

The new settlers thought of themselves as hardy, healthy types. They loved the new challenges hard winters had to offer. A big part of the Christmas season was spent outdoors. People played in the snow even on Christmas Day. Christmas dinner was eaten shortly after noon. In the afternoon people went for rides in sleighs and cutters. Some played lacrosse; others went ice-sailing or ice-fishing on the lakes. Tobogganing and sledding were popular with both children and adults.

Skating was the most popular Christmas outdoor activity. Children and adults went out to skate on frozen lakes. Sometimes even the family pets shared in the fun!

These hardy snowshoe club members race through the forest at night carrying torches.

People of all ages had snowball fights.

Which young man will be brave enough to take the mistletoe challenge?

The horns announce the coming of the "taffy pullers".

Love and marriage, Christmas style!

Christmas spirit turned the thoughts of young men and women to love. There was not a lot of time for romance during the other seasons of the year. There was always too much work to do. At Christmas, however, the attentions of people were focused on social events. When people are relaxed and having fun they start to listen to their feelings. Often, those feelings whispered romance and marriage!

Pulling for love

The French settlers started the romance season with taffy pulling on November 25. Taffy pulling was held in honor of Saint Catherine, the patron saint of single women. Taffy pulling allowed young men and women to meet each other before the start of the Christmas season.

The taffy pulling bee was similar to the other bees held by the settlers. There was always a job to be done first and lots of fun to be had afterwards. In this case,

the young people boiled molasses into a syrup. After the syrup was cooled, it formed a sticky taffy. The taffy was then pulled into long strips. It tasted really good. The taffy pull ended with a big dinner and lots of dancing. Many men and women met their future wives and husbands at one of these taffy pulls.

Christmas kisses

There were many parties during the Christmas season. Dances were held starting early in December and continuing through Christmas. Parlor games were often played at these parties and dances.

Mistletoe and kissing boughs hung in many homes. Young men and women were supposed to kiss each other while standing under either one. Mistletoe only grows in mild climates, so it had to be ordered at the store at Christmas. Those who could not buy any mistletoe made kissing boughs out of evergreens and apples.

Here comes the Christmas bride!

Race home and be the first to party!

A whole week to wed!

Christmas romances often led to Christmas weddings. The parties held for the wedding couple lasted well over a week. The Christmas season was the only time that most people were free to attend the parties. Most of the weddings of the time were like the one described below.

Invitations in person

During the week before the wedding, the fathers of the bride and groom each invited his own guests in person. The fathers traveled to the homes of neighbors to tell them the good news. They informed the guests of the times of the wedding and parties.

Race home, but do not pass the bride!

The night before the wedding a dance was held at the bride's house. The next morning the wedding procession lined up at the house of the bride. The sleighs and carioles carrying the guests escorted the bride and groom to the church. The wedding party led the procession. After the wedding was over, the guests raced each other back to the home of the bride. It was considered bad manners to pass the bridal party during the race. Many of the guests ended up in the snow. Somehow, everyone managed to arrive at the home of the bride in time for dinner and dancing.

Rest up to party again!

The bridal party and guests rested up for a few days until the parties started again. The Sunday after the wedding was again reserved for the bride and groom. The couple, dressed in their wedding clothes, drove to church, followed by the guests. The horses were decorated with colored ribbons. On that Sunday, the sermon was about marriage. The guests returned to the bride's house for dinner.

Welcome home, new daughter!

The following day, smaller parties were held in honor of the bride and groom. Then, the whole wedding party went to the home of the groom. The father of the groom welcomed the bride into his home. After that, everyone celebrated and danced until the wee hours of the morning.

The men come a-calling

New Year's Day was one of the most exciting days of the Christmas season for both young men and women. All day long, men called on women to wish them a Happy New Year. The men came on snowshoes, on horses, by sleigh and on foot. They came alone and in groups. They stayed at each home for about fifteen minutes. The ladies, waiting with great excitement, offered their callers tea, coffee, sandwiches and wine. As the gentlemen were ready to leave, they left their calling cards behind in the hallway of the house. In the next few days, the girls compared the numbers of cards they had received.

Miss Pegu, I'm bragging to you!

The men also bragged about how many calls they had made. Men in the government even published the number of their New Year's visits in the paper. One eager gentleman caller even made up a rhyme to recite during his calls. Each time he made a new call, he changed the name and the number in his jingle. This is what he said:

"Howd'ye do, Miss Pegu. Happy New Year! Can't stay a minute. Made seventy-six calls this morning; got thirty more to make. Adoo! Adoo!"

And they accused girls of bragging!

The bride and groom start off the dancing.

Here comes caller number twenty-six!

It is a terrible duty to have to catch your old pet, the goose, and give it to your mother to cook for Christmas dinner!

Christmas preparations often started as early as Thanksgiving. This is an apple-bee. Friends and neighbors first peel and then core the apples. Some of the apples are squeezed into juice, which will later become cider. Many of the apples will be sliced and made into pies for Christmas. After the work is done, a dinner and dance will follow.

Hard preparations for happy celebrations

It took many months to prepare for Christmas. Winter was a special time for the settlers because it was the only time they were free from their farming chores. They still had to look after the animals in the farmyard, but they didn't have to look after the crops in the fields.

Christmas celebrations often lasted for several weeks. The Christmas season was the party season. When people prepared for it, they really prepared. Everyone wanted to make Christmas a time to remember. People tried to outdo each other. Both the men and the women had a lot of jobs to do to get ready for Christmas. The rich settlers had servants to do

their work for them. But most of the other settlers did their own chores.

In those days men did certain jobs and women did others. However, there were times when everyone in the community got together and helped a neighbor to do a job. These get-togethers were called "bees". There were threshing bees, apple bees, barn-raising bees and quilting bees. When there was a difficult job to be done, a bee was the quickest and easiest way to do it. Bees were fun because there was always a lot of socializing and food. And, there was dancing after the work was done! People worked together to make their Christmases hard to forget.

Mopping the kitchen floor.

Putting their backs into washing.

Dividing up the pre-Christmas chores

The mince pie goes into the oven.

WHAT THE WOMEN WILL DO *

- Clean the house
- Wash the tablecloths, rugs and curtains
- Press the best quilts
- Make new clothes for every member of the family to wear at the Christmas parties
- Make jams and preserves
- Choose the best vegetables and fruits and store them separately from the other food
- Prepare those pies and cakes which can be made ahead of time
- Prepare the sausages and roasts
- Make soups
- Make mincemeat for pies
- Prepare the plum pudding
- Set aside the best spices and herbs

*In the early settler days men and women had separate jobs. Today men and women often do the same jobs.

Plowing a path to the church.

WHAT THE MEN WILL DO

- Cut firewood for the fireplaces
- Bring the flour home from the mill
- Hunt or slaughter the animals for roasting
- Smoke or salt the meat
- Prepare the sausages, bacon and roasts for cooking
- Repair, paint and varnish the sleighs
- Polish the Christmas sleighbells
- Check over the harnesses
- Air out the bear, wolf and moose blankets in the sleighs
- Brush down the horses
- Run errands for the women
- Clear the road to the church
- Chop evergreens for decorations

Taking home the flour from the mill.

Moose nose for Christmas!

The children parade into the dining room with the part of the dinner they like best – the pudding! And the pudding is pulled by the part of the dinner they like the second best – the turkey! A good pudding was made with raisins, spices, eggs, flour, meat and plums.

The cleaning, stuffing and cooking of the turkey occupied all available hands.

A feast to remember all year!

The settlers would put so much food on the table that Christmas dinner would last for hours. The usual Christmas table in those days "groaned" with the weight of the food on it. It was not surprising that the preparation of the Christmas dinner took months to complete.

The following Christmas dinner menu was suggested in a cookbook of that time.

Bring on the pudding!

CHRISTMAS DINNER 1842

Oyster Soup
Boiled Turbot
Roast Turkey   Cranberry Sauce
Roast Beef   Boiled Pork
Mashed and Browned Potatoes
Onions in Cream Sauce
Tomatoes
Chicken Pie
Rice Croquettes
Plum Pudding   Foaming Sauce
Mince Pies
Raspberry Trifle
Walnuts
Celery
Crackers   Cheese
Fruit
Coffee

If you did not want turkey for Christmas, the meat market had interesting alternatives. How about venison, which is deer meat, or a tasty rat steak!

Buy, bag or shoot your dinner

It was usual to find several roasts of meat at the early Christmas dinner table. Some of the favorites were roasts of goose, beef, duck, pork, chicken, buffalo, moose and, of course, the old favorite, turkey. Some of the settlers who lived in or near the cities were able to buy most of their meat at a market. But most had to rely on raising their own animals. Those who were out in the wilderness had plenty of game to choose from. All they had to do was to shoot it.

Tricky turkeys make delicious dinners

Wild birds, such as pheasants or turkeys, were trapped with bags. The hunter had to imitate the mating call of the bird, and then jump the bird as it came near, trapping it in a big cloth bag. Bagging wild turkeys was tricky because turkeys were fast! Turkeys were new to the settlers. There were no turkeys in England or Europe. The settlers loved the taste so much, that they decided their relatives should also try some. A smart businessman shipped some turkeys to England. The English domesticated the turkey. The domesticated bird was moister than the wild turkey. It was certainly easier to catch! But many people said that nothing tasted as wonderful as the old wild turkey!

This settler did not have the patience to bag his turkey. One shot, one turkey!

Turkey's done!

Wish upon a stir!

Christmas pudding took five weeks to make. It was prepared in November on "Stir Up Sunday", the last Sunday before Advent. The whole family had a turn at stirring up the pudding. Everyone made a wish as they stirred. Sometimes poems were recited as one stirred.

Here is an example of such a poem.

When merry, frosty Christmas comes,
Mamma takes currants, peel and plums;
Spice, raisins, flour, and eggs she takes,
And with them all a pudding makes;
So we are glad when Christmas comes
And brings us puddings full of plums.

A pudding filled with Christmas spirit

Christmas dinner was not Christmas dinner without plum pudding! In almost every Christmas issue of newspapers and magazines of the time there was at least one picture of the family either preparing, serving or enjoying their Christmas pudding. The Christmas pudding was the symbol of Christmas for the early settler. It was a tie to the past. The ingredients of the pudding were not as important as the spirit which went into preparing and serving it to the family and friends.

Plum pudding started out as a kind of porridge called "frumenty". Frumenty was eaten during the fast before Christmas. Many Christians fasted each year before the birthday of Jesus Christ. This period of fasting is called Advent. The Advent porridge was later mixed with sausages called "hackin". This mixture of frumenty and hackin was the birth of the plum pudding! The first plum puddings contained meat, eggs, porridge, currants or raisins and other fruit. Later, there was more of the fruit and nuts and less meat.

Often coins were put inside the pudding, along with a button. This button was called the "bachelor button". It was said that the person who got the button in his or her share of the pudding would remain unmarried. The stirred pudding was kept in a big pot for five weeks. It was steamed in a cloth or mold on Christmas Day and served with a rum or brandy sauce. Everyone looked forward to the moment that mother would walk into the room with the pudding all in flames. The warm rum or brandy, which had been poured over the pudding and lit, danced in flames to the tune of the leaping hearts of those about to do justice to every tasty morsel!

Supper is over at the children's party. The crackers have been exploded. As Daniel the dog does his little dance on the table, some of the girls are getting ready to go home.

A change for children

Parents began to fuss over their children.

It wasn't fun to be a child two hundred years ago. Children were meant to be "seen and not heard" then. Children were judged by how much work they could do as children and adults. Both men and women wanted to have boy babies. Sons would grow up and help their fathers to work on the farm or to take over the family business. Boys usually stayed with the family. Girls grew up to marry and become mothers. They would often live with the families of their husbands. Today very few boys or girls stay with their families after they marry.

Many children died because of illnesses that had no cures in those days. Many children were treated badly by their parents. In the early cities children often wandered the streets without a home. It was not unusual to find children working long hours at very low wages. Farm children had a lot of chores to do too. Few people seemed to care about the hardships children had to suffer because life was not easy for anyone in those days!

Children are allowed to be children

About one hundred and thirty years ago people started to change their feelings about children. Newspapers showed pictures of families having good times together. There were pictures of cute children in the magazines and papers. It became popular to love one's children and to fuss over them. People suddenly started treating their children as children, instead of as little adults. Children began to play more and to work less. The papers continually published poems and stories about poor and homeless children.

The following poem was printed in the paper around Christmas time about one hundred and twenty years ago. What is the message of the poem?

Christmas has come, with gifts and toys,
For little girls as well as boys.
Mary has got a picture-book,
At which she and her sister look;
And Jane has got a gilded fan,
And something nice has come for Ann;
Baby has got a neat doll, dressed
In scarlet coat and bright blue vest –
Mary and Jane, and Ann I know,
When Christmas comes with frost & snow
Will think upon the girls and boys
Who get no pretty Christmas toys
Who suffer want, and cold, and care,
And help them both with alms and prayer.

Christmas becomes a time for children

Christmas became an especially important time for children. Families tried to outdo each other in the number of gifts they gave their children. Christmas soon became the most special time of the year for children. The Christmas that used to be for adults changed almost overnight to a Christmas for children. Santa Claus, Christmas stockings and the Christmas tree all became important about this time. Parties were no longer for adults. Instead, all efforts were made so that children would enjoy themselves at Christmas. And because of all the special efforts to make children happy at Christmas, the spirit of Christmas love seemed to last the whole year long!

In the early days of our country, the government did not help people who had misfortunes. This boy's mother and father died from tuberculosis, a disease of the lungs. He has no relatives to care for him. He must beg for food from door to door. Although people didn't help the poor all year long, at Christmas everyone was much more generous. People visited the sick, the poor and even the convicts. The boy in this picture will probably get a good meal today because it is Christmas.

This is Saint Nicholas, holding the Christ Child in his arms. Saint Nicholas was a bishop in the country that is now Turkey.

The changing faces of Santa Claus

Santa Claus was not well known in the early days of our country. He had many different names, such as Father Christmas, Kris Kringle, Bellsnickle and Saint Nicholas. People didn't know exactly what he looked like. Some said he was tall with a long beard and wore the clothing of a bishop. Others thought of him as a jolly little elf.

How Santa got here

No one was quite sure how Santa Claus delivered his presents. Newspapers showed Santa coming by horse, reindeer, moose, on snowshoes and by bicycle. Some people even thought giant turkeys took Santa from house to house.

Saint Nick, Santa from Europe

There were many stories about Saint Nick. Each country in Europe had its own beliefs about Saint Nicholas. He usually came to bring gifts for children on December sixth. He filled children's stockings or shoes with candies and small gifts. Sometimes he left a spanking switch if the children had been bad. Saint Nicholas had a helper named Black Peter. Sometimes this helper was called Bellsnickle. He could be mean!

Christkindl becomes Kris Kringle

German people believed that a messenger named *Christkindl* brought presents from Baby Jesus on Christmas Eve. Christkindl was a young female angel. The name "Christkindl" became another name for Santa Claus in North America. Many people called Santa "Kris Kringle".

This Santa appeared in the newspaper one early Christmas. He is different from the Santa in the red suit that appears in the papers today. Instead of a stocking cap, he wears a turban. He is tiny and thin. However, in some ways he resembles today's Santa. In what ways? What do the pictures around the sides tell us about Christmas in those early days?

HIS droll little
mouth was
drawn up like a bow,
And the beard on his chin
was as white as the snow.
The stump of a pipe he held
tight in his teeth,
And the smoke, it encircled his
head like a wreath:
He had a broad face, and a
little round belly,
That shook, when he laughed,
like a bowl full of jelly;
He was chubby and plump, a right
jolly old elf;
And I laughed, when I saw him, in
spite of myself.

Visits from different Santas

In 1823, over 150 years ago, a man named Dr. Clement Moore wrote a poem called "A Visit From Saint Nicholas". You probably know this poem as "The Night Before Christmas". Dr. Moore described what Santa looked like in this poem. He said Saint Nicholas was jolly, fat and round. Even though many people read this poem they still did not have an idea of what Santa looked like. The pictures that appeared in the newspapers showed many different Santas. These early Santas did not look much like the Santa Clement Moore had written about.

In this old photograph, Santa is packing his bag for the trip south on Christmas Eve. This Santa is much more like the Santa we know today, but he is still a little on the thin side. How is he different from the Santa on the opposite page?

Finally our Santa arrives

An artist named Thomas Nast began to draw pictures of Santa Claus around 1863. Nast's drawings appeared in "Harper's Weekly" a New York journal. Other artists from other newspapers started to copy his drawings of Santa Claus. Thomas Nast's Santa looked like the Santa we know today. He was fat, had a full, white beard and rosy cheeks. Nast started calling him "Santa Claus" instead of all the other names he had, such as Kris Kringle and Saint Nicholas.

No one had ever thought about where Santa lived. Thomas Nast gave Santa a home on the North Pole. The North Pole did not belong to any country. All children could be visited by Santa, no matter where they lived or what their government was!

From the pile of letters on the left, it seems that Santa will have a light load.

Jim wonders whether Santa will fill the huge stocking he is nailing up.

Mark and Ned catch a glimpse of Santa on their rooftop.

Martin Luther and his family celebrate Christmas a new way, with a Christmas tree. German settlers carried on the tradition of bringing evergreen trees into their homes and decorating them. This custom was called "the German way of celebrating Christmas" in the early days.

The Dear Old Tree
BY LUELLA WILSON SMITH

There's a dear old tree,
an evergreen tree,
And it blossoms once a year.
'Tis loaded with fruit from top to root,
And it brings to all good cheer.

For its blossoms bright are small candles white
And its fruit is dolls and toys
And they all are free for both you and me
If we're good little girls & boys.

The bright and beautiful tree

The custom of putting up Christmas trees came from Germany. Martin Luther, the founder of the Lutheran Church, wanted to show his children the beauty of the night that Jesus Christ was born. He put an evergreen tree into the nursery. He placed the tree behind a nativity scene. A nativity scene has carved figures showing Joseph, Mary, the shepherds and the wise men in the stable where Jesus was born. The candles on the branches of the tree looked like stars in the darkness. The stars shone down over the cradle of Jesus.

Soon many German people had trees in their homes at Christmas. Decorations were added. The German people who settled here had trees in their homes long before it became a custom that other settlers followed.

Santa Claus and the Christmas tree brought about the new Christmas for children. If you look at the pictures earlier on in this book, you will see that Christmas was an adult event. However, with the coming of the Christmas tree, Christmas changed to a Christmas for children. There were more and more children's parties, and gift-giving became an important part of Christmas.

Toys were usually not wrapped, but placed on or under the tree. At this large family gathering, the host father is giving out the presents to his sons, daughters, nieces and nephews. Some of the children are playing with their new toys, while others are enjoying the company of their visiting grandfather. Christmas was truly a joyful occasion for children!

This tree may fall over from the number of presents on it. How many different presents can you discover?

These two girls, many years ago, snuck out of their beds to admire the tree that their parents decorated and found that Santa had already paid his visit!

A new Christmas symbol

Queen Victoria, the famous Queen of England 1837 to 1901, married a German named Prince Albert. He brought the German custom of decorating Christmas trees to England. He put up a tree for his wife and children one Christmas Eve in the 1840 s. The picture of his family around the Christmas tree appeared in the newspapers in England, the United States and Canada. Soon everyone on both continents decorated trees at Christmas.

Delightful, but dangerous!

The first North American Christmas trees were decorated with candles, fruit, pine cones, cookies, lozenges and home-made ornaments. Later small gifts were put right on the trees. The father of the family distributed these gifts to the children.

There were many decorations on Christmas trees, including candles. People kept pails of water near the tree to put out fires caused by the candles. Many Christmas trees burned down and many more fell down. But the custom of putting trees up has never died. The Christmas tree is one of the most important symbols of our Christmas today – a Christmas that has brought joy to so many children.

Laura dreams of all the wonderful toys she might find under the tree in the morning.

Grandma is knitting warm socks for her grandson John. She is putting a lot of love into her gift. John will be happy!

The settlers who lived in or near a village could buy or order their gifts at the General Store. Amanda finds a strong cane for Dad.

Gifts for all!

At first the early settlers made their gifts by hand. Mothers made stockings, nightshirts and scarves for their children. Fathers made blocks, sleds and wooden horses. As villages and towns grew, more gifts were bought rather than made. In the country gifts could be ordered at the General Store. In the towns and cities many types of gifts were available in big department stores. Christmas became commercial soon after Santa became well-known.

Many city children worked in workshops and factories for low wages. These girls would probably love to own a doll!

However, the children who received the dolls often neither appreciated the dolls, nor the hard work of the doll-makers.

Children loved magic lantern shows. These lucky children will soon own the magic lantern projector balanced on Santa's head.

Fire engines were popular gifts.

Every child loved to play board games, especially ones to do with Christmas!

Toys for boys and girls

As cities became larger, department stores appeared. Their windows were filled with exciting presents.

Santa admires the clothes that Mary has sewn for her doll. Mary used the miniature sewing machine that Santa brought her.

Dolls, dolls, dolls

Every little girl dreamed of getting a doll for Christmas. There were beautiful dolls then, as there are now. Many of the old dolls from that time have been copied and are now being sold for a lot of money. Most of the first dolls were grown-up dolls. They were dressed in adult clothes. Some even wore corsets and bustles. Corsets were worn by ladies to make their waists look thinner. Bustles made ladies' skirts stick out at the back. The dolls were dressed in the top fashions of the day. Baby dolls became popular a few years later. Some little girls had big doll houses with many dolls. Others were happy to have corn husk dolls made by their mothers.

Best loved gifts

Miniature tea sets were another popular gift. Little girls loved to have tea parties for their dolls. The tea sets were made of real china. There were no plastic toys in those days. Small sewing machines and cooking stoves were very popular too. Girls could make their own doll clothes and cookies to leave for Santa Claus.

Boys played with wooden trains, circus sets, soldiers, hobby horses and wagons. Fathers carved wonderful home-made toys out of wood. Many ready-made toys could be bought in shops.

In the early days, children were not allowed to play with toys on Sundays. Sunday was a day for church, for prayer and for reading the Bible. However, one toy that was allowed was the Noah's Ark. It was loved by both boys and girls. The Ark was made of wood and had two each of many different animals. Both boys and girls wanted Noah's Arks for Christmas.

This poor mother is sad because she finds it difficult to explain to her daughter on Christmas morning why Santa did not fill her daughter's stocking with presents. While many children received presents and had large Christmas meals, others received no presents and went hungry.

This old Christmas card is a copy of Henry Cole's first Christmas card. It has a picture of a painter on the bottom right hand corner, so we can assume that it was sent to Henry Cole by the man who colored his cards, Joseph Cundall. Or could it be J.C. Horsley?

Christmas cards, a new custom

The first settlers in North America never sent Christmas cards to each other as we do today. It took weeks for letters to go from one place to another in those days. To get a letter from Europe could take up to a year. But it was not because the mail was slow that people did not send cards. No one had ever thought of the idea!

Cole's big idea

In 1843, about 140 years ago, an Englishman named Henry Cole had a problem. He was so busy that he had no time to write letters to his friends at Christmas. He hired an artist, J.C. Horsley, to design a card for him. He had one thousand cards printed from Mr. Horsley's design. Joseph Cundall colored each card by hand.

Mr. Cundall was a shop owner in England. He sold the cards that Henry Cole did not send. The price of the cards was very high. The idea of sending Christmas cards was born! However, it did not catch on for a long time.

The idea catches on

Years later contests were held to find good designs for Christmas cards. With better printing machines, people were able to make beautiful, colorful cards. The prices of the cards were a lot less too! The post office helped to make sending Christmas cards more popular by charging only half the postage during the Christmas season.

A boy tries out Santa's present in a Louis Prang Christmas card.

Canadian sweethearts flash down a steep hill, the wind whipping their scarves.

Louis Prang, master card maker

English people sent Christmas cards to relatives in the United States and Canada. The custom of sending cards became popular almost overnight in both countries. Each year in Boston Louis Prang held contests for the best Christmas card designs. He was one of the first Americans to print them. Louis Prang's printing process was so good that he could print as many as fifteen colors on one card. The printed cards looked exactly the same as the original artwork they were printed from.

Popular scenes

The most popular Canadian Christmas cards had winter themes. The cards showed people sleighing, snowshoeing, tobogganing and skating. Many of the designs for the cards were taken from the works of famous Canadian artists, such as Cornelius Krieghoff and William Bartlett. Some of the cards had silk fringe borders.

Andrea chooses a card at the General Store with Judie, the storekeeper's daughter.

There is lots of good food for hungry stomachs at réveillon. This French settler family celebrates the birth of Christ with a huge meal after Midnight Mass.

The customs of different settlers

French celebrations

The French settlers celebrated Christmas as a very religious holiday. They went to Midnight Mass on Christmas Eve. After the mass, families feasted late into the night. The dinner after midnight was called *réveillon*. The food at reveillon included meat pies, meat balls, fowl, suet pudding, stews and cakes. For many years the partying was saved until New Year's Eve. However, as the French and English settlers lived together, some of the French customs changed a little.

When the first French settlers celebrated Christmas, they did not give presents to their children until New Year's Eve. Later on, the presents were brought by *Père Noël*, the French name for Santa, after Midnight Mass on Christmas Eve. Gift-giving became, and still is, a part of réveillon.

New Year's Eve was celebrated by dancing and partying until dawn. On New Year's Day fathers blessed their children, starting with the oldest one. Everyone spent the day at either the father's or the grandfather's house.

German contributions

The custom of putting up Christmas trees came from Germany. German settlers also introduced us to Santa Claus and Christmas stockings. Germans hung Advent wreaths from the ceiling and lit one candle each Sunday before Christmas. Many people light Advent wreaths today. The Advent Calendar also originated in Germany. Children love to open a different window each day before Christmas.

The whole family comes to grandfather's home on New Year's Day. He blesses the children in order from the eldest to the youngest. Everyone spends the day together in feast and fun.

Mennonite ways

The Mennonites, a religious group from Germany, had some interesting customs. They left plates with their names on them out on Christmas Eve. In the morning the plates were filled with fruit and nuts. It was also believed that if a girl looked into the mirror on January the sixth when she was alone, she would see the face of the young man she would marry.

Hogmanay from Scotland

Christmas Day was a religious day for the Scots. There was no partying or dancing. The day was reserved for going to church. Hogmanay, or New Year's Eve, was the time for fun. There was feasting, dancing and celebrating. Just after midnight, the men went "first footing". Whoever entered a house first after midnight would bring good or bad luck to the family who lived there. If a man with dark hair came, the family would have good luck for the coming year. If a man with red hair was

Yule Logs were burned by settlers from England and Scandinavia. The Yule Log custom did not last for long here.

New Year's calling became a fashionable affair, popular with people of all backgrounds. The custom was carried out for over two hundred years. It is still practiced by many politicians.

Dutch children imagined Santa to look like this. Why is he holding those sticks?

the first to enter, the luck would be bad. Women first footers also brought bad luck. It was a custom for first footers to bring a gift.

"First footing" changed into the custom of New Year's calling. The callers came on New Year's Day, instead of on New Year's Eve. Settlers of all different backgrounds took part in New Year's calling.

Sleipner from Holland

The children of the Dutch settlers believed that an eight-footed horse called Sleipner brought Saint Nicholas on December the sixth. Children filled their shoes with hay for Sleipner. Sleipner left gifts in the place of the hay for those children who were good. The bad children got spanking switches.

From Sweden and the Ukraine

Swedish settlers also had a similar custom. They left hay in corners of the room and hid candies and nuts in the hay. Ukrainians also decorated the Christmas table with hay to remind themselves of the humble birth of Jesus Christ.

Glossary

backwoods *heavily wooded, thinly settled area*

bee *a gathering of people working together*

blindman's bluff *a game – a blindfolded person tries to catch and name the person caught*

bush *woods*

bustle *a frame which gives extra fullness to the upper back of a skirt*

cardamon *ground seeds from an Asiatic plant – used as a spice*

cariole *a type of sleigh*

charades *a game – person acts out a phrase or sentence in pantomime*

chores *small, routine jobs around house or farm*

cock-fighting *a fight between game-cocks*

corn husk doll *a doll made from the green outer leaves of corn*

corset *an undergarment used to hold in the waist*

critter *country word meaning animal or creature*

croquette *a small, deep fried cake of minced food*

cutter *a small single-horse sleigh*

frontier *wilderness beyond a settled area*

frumenty *a porridge made of wheat boiled in milk*

fur trading post *a store or fort in the wilderness where furs were traded for other products*

General Store *a country store which sold everything a settler might have needed*

ginger *a root from Asia often ground into a powder – a spice*

hackin *Scottish sausages*

hallowed *holy*

harvest *the time to gather crops*

Hogmanay *Scottish New Year's Eve*

holly *an evergreen shrub or tree with shiny red berries and spiny, prickly leaves – a Christmas decoration*

incense *a wood or gum which produces a pleasant smoke when burned*

kissing bough *a sphere covered in evergreens from which apples hang – couples kissed underneath it*

logger *lumberjack*

mistletoe *a shrub with white berries. It is customary to kiss underneath a branch of it at Christmas.*

nigh *near*

nineteenth century *1801 to 1900*

orris root *a fragrant root used in perfumes*

ox-cart *a small wagon pulled by oxen*

pantry *a small, cool room where food and dishes were stored*

parson *a clergyman*

pomander *a fruit covered in cloves and other spices which when dried creates a lovely aroma*

preserves *food that was bottled or salted to keep from going bad*

repose *rest*

trapper *one who traps animals for their fur*

trifle *a dessert of sherry-soaked cake topped with jam, custard and whipped cream*

tuberculosis *a disease that destroys the lungs*

turbot *a delicious flat fish which tastes like sole*

voyageur *a person employed by fur companies to transport furs and supplies between remote places*

wilderness *unsettled, uncultivated land*

Index

Acknowledgements

Library of Congress
Dover Publications
Scugog Shores Museum, Port Perry
Harper's Weekly
Black Creek Pioneer Village
Frank Leslie's Illustrated Magazine
Metropolitan Toronto Library
Illustrated London News
Canadian Illustrated News

15 LB Printed in the U.S.A. 9